concept.

AUG - - 2003

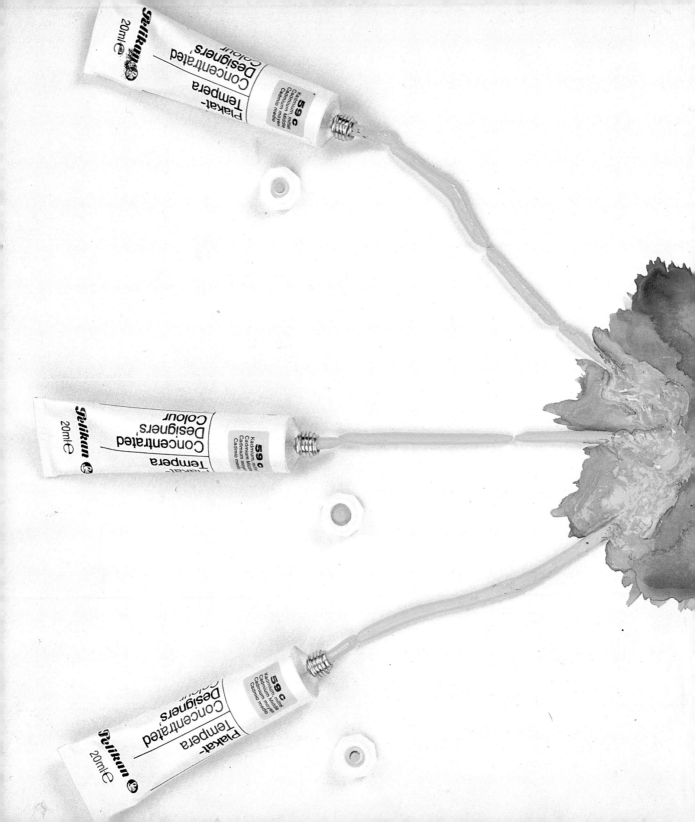

je c.1

© 1990 Franklin Watts

Franklin Watts Inc.
387 Park Avenue South
New York, N.Y. 10016

Library of Congress Cataloging-in-Publication Data
Pluckrose, Henry Arthur.
    Change it! / Henry Pluckrose.
        p.   cm. — (Ways to)
    Summary: Color photographs and simple text explore different ways
of saying "Change it".
    ISBN 0-531-14064-4
    1. Vocabulary—Juvenile literature.   [1. Vocabulary.   I. Title.
II. Series: Pluckrose, Henry Arthur.   Ways to.
PE1449.P575   1990
428.1—dc20   89-70746
                                                    CIP AC

Editor: Kate Petty
Design: K & Co

Artwork: Aziz Khan

Printed in Italy by
G. Canale S.p.A., Turin

Ways to....

CHANGE *it!*

Henry Pluckrose

Photography by Chris Fairclough

FRANKLIN WATTS

New York • London • Sydney • Toronto

What do we mean by change? Which one of these things...

has been used to
make each of
these?

How are things changed?

To make a cake we mix the ingredients together.

The mixture is baked in a hot oven.

The heat turns the raw mixture into a cake.

Jello is made with boiling water. It sets into a shape as it cools.

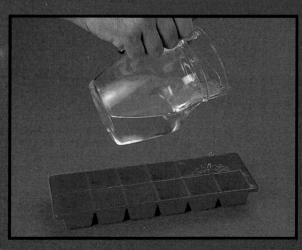

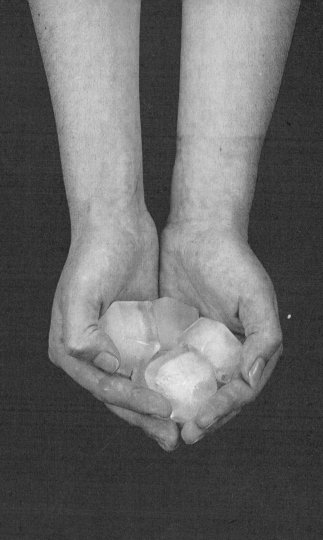

Water changes to ice when it gets very cold. How do you melt ice?

Water can change dry powder into a liquid.

Which is easier to paint with?

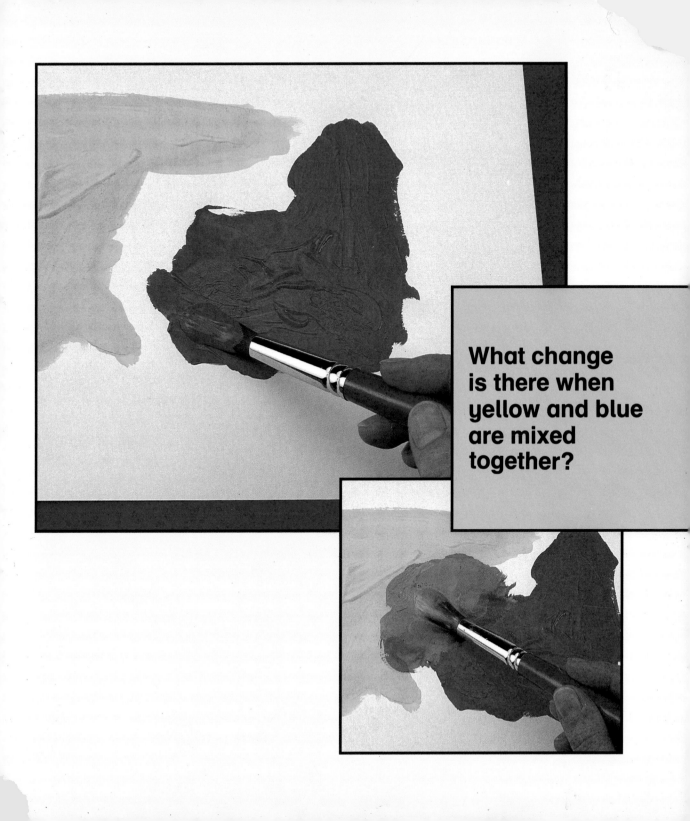

What change is there when yellow and blue are mixed together?

Some things change their shape. A bag looks different when filled with groceries.

Balloons change shape when filled with air.

Clothes can look a different shape...

...with people
inside them...

Some things change as they grow.
Can you match these pictures?

eggs

acorn

baby

bulb

daffodils

old person

oak tree

duck

We need tools to change trees like this...

into wooden
furniture or
wooden toys.

sheep-shearing

spinning

dyeing

**Many things are
done to change
wool from sheep
into clothes.
The sheep has
to be sheared
and the wool...**

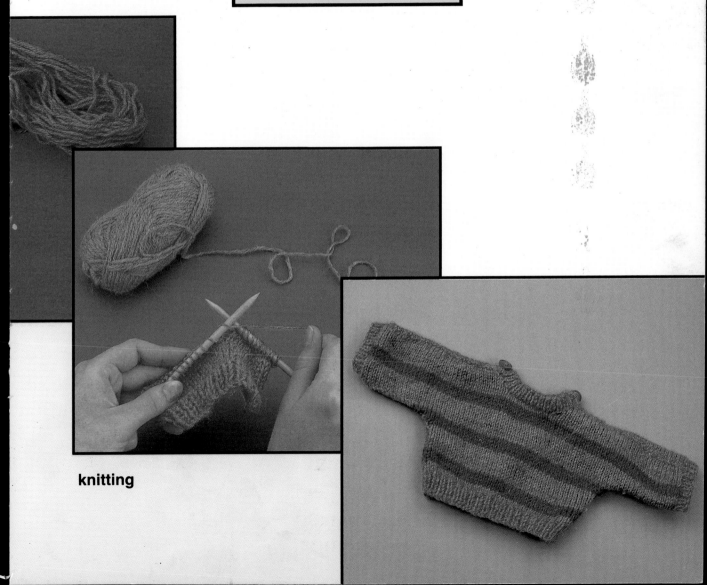

**...spun,
...dyed,
and knitted
into the
right shape.**

knitting

Most of these machines help cooks to turn raw ingredients into something to eat or drink.

Which is the odd one out?

dough

There are many ways in which things change. Can you match these pictures?

eggs

summer

milk

winter

cheese

bread

toad

Things to do

● Changing colors

Put a wet blob of yellow paint on a piece of paper. Mix some blue paint into it. What happens?

Put a wet blob of red paint on a piece of paper. Mix some yellow paint into it. What happens?

What new colors are made if you mix
— black and white?

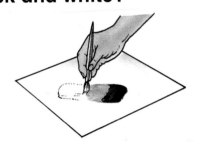

— red and blue?

— yellow with red and then with blue?

● Looking through a color

Find some colored cellophane (candy wrappers will do well).
Close one eye and look through a piece of red cellophane. What do you notice?

Find some other colors to look through — green, yellow or blue. What changes are there in the colors of the things you are looking at?

• How many times a day do you

— change your shoes?
— change your clothes?
— change your seat?

• Changing a flat shape

Cut a piece of paper into four pieces, like this

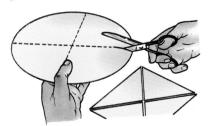

or this

Now rearrange the pieces to make different patterns. How many different patterns can you make?

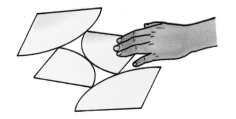

• Changing a solid shape

Find a piece of modeling clay. Can you shape it into ...?

a ball	a worm
a bridge	a face
a brick	a plate
a house	a bathtub

• What do we mean by...?

Changing hands
Changing money
Changing places
Changing sides
Changing trains
A change of heart
A change in the weather

Words about changing

alter	improve
become	make
bend	melt
camouflage	mold
color	rearrange
decay	repair
decrease	reshape
develop	shift
dye	turn
grow	twist

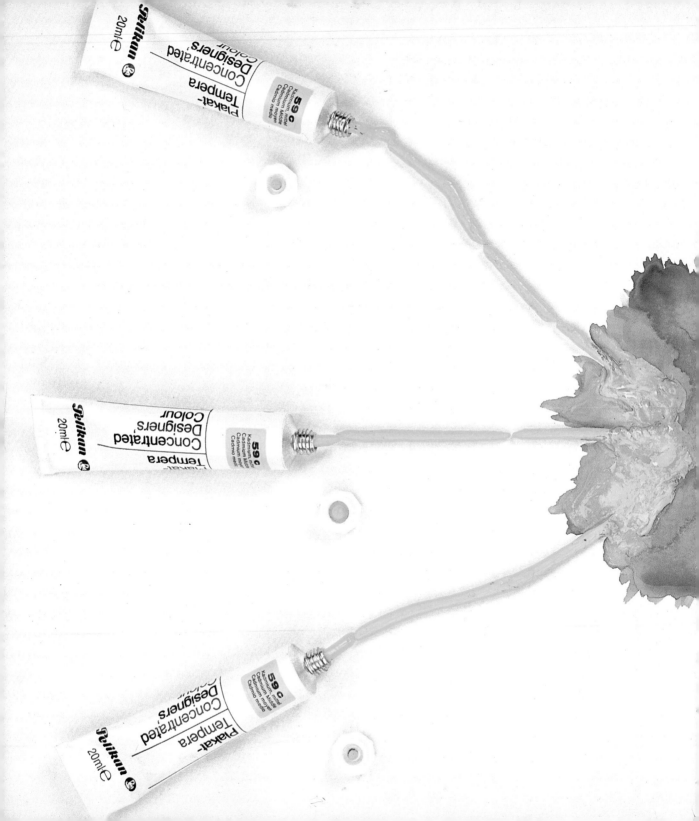

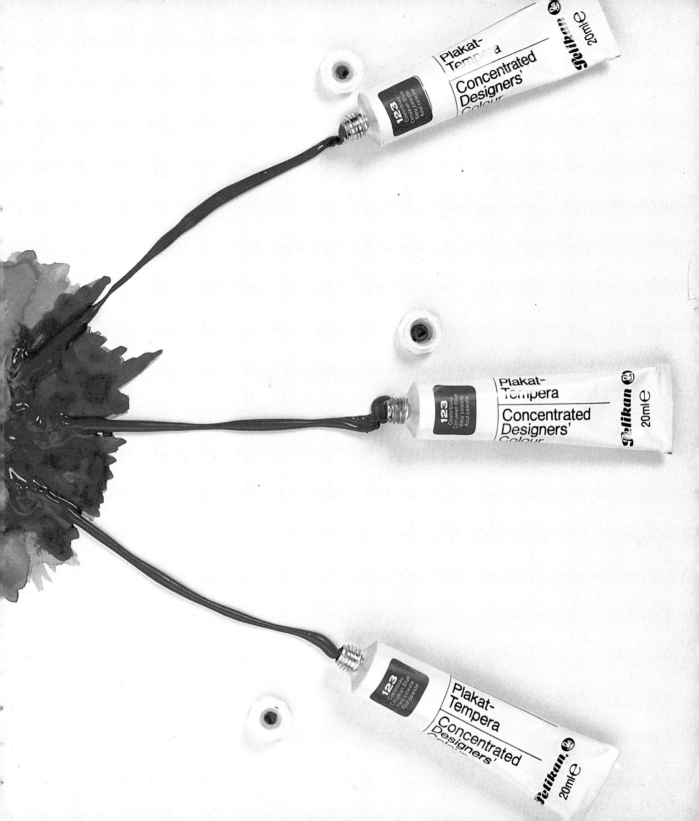